Pin It!

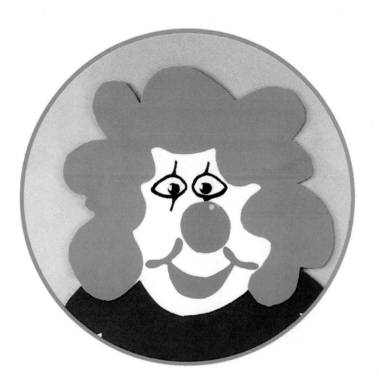

Written by Barbara Rosen
Photographs by John Paul Endress

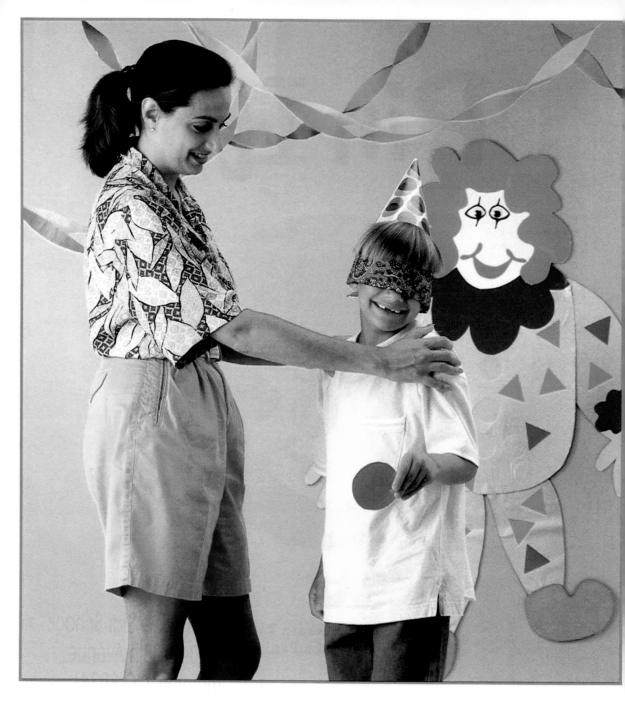

Spin, spin, spin.

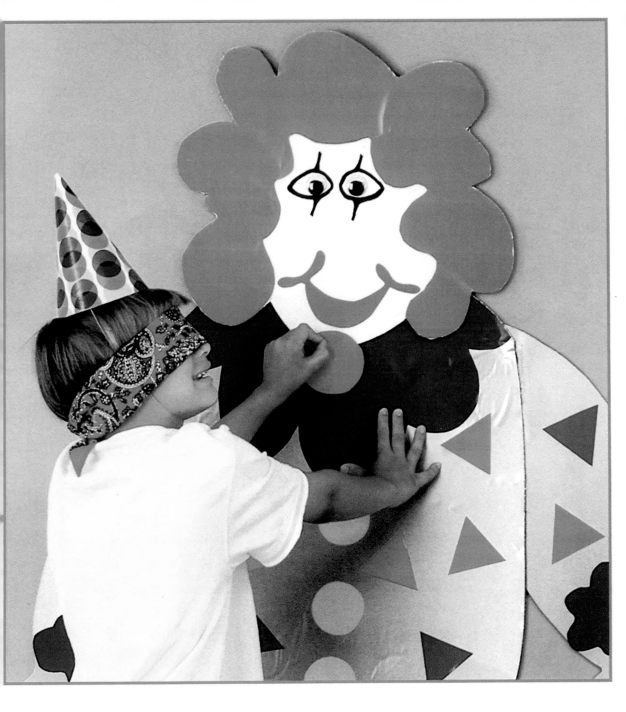

Pin it on the chin.

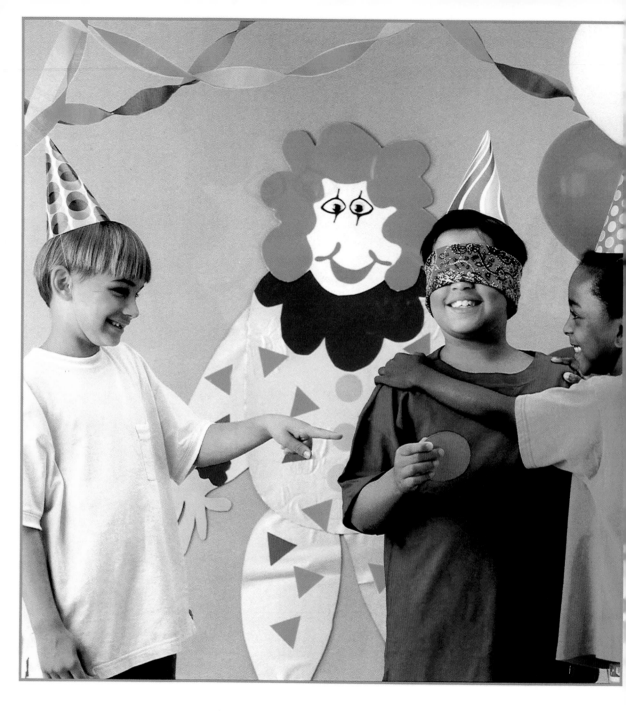

Spin, spin, spin.

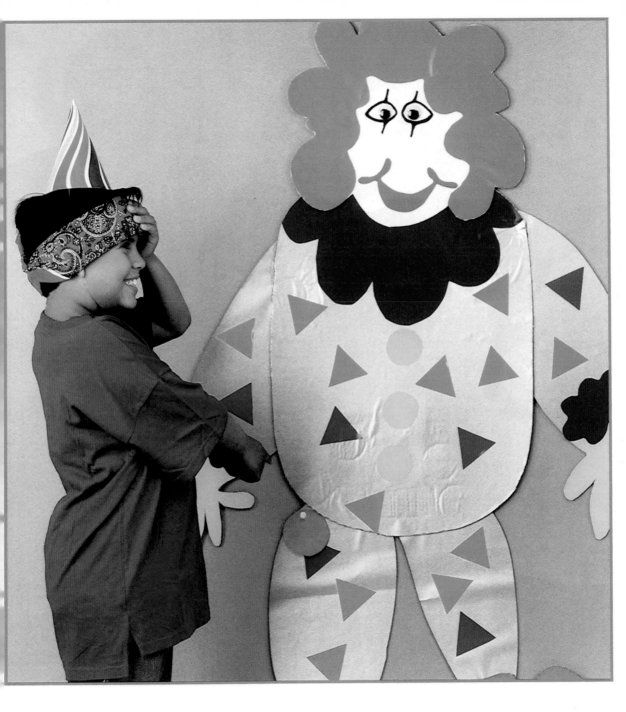

Pin it on the leg.

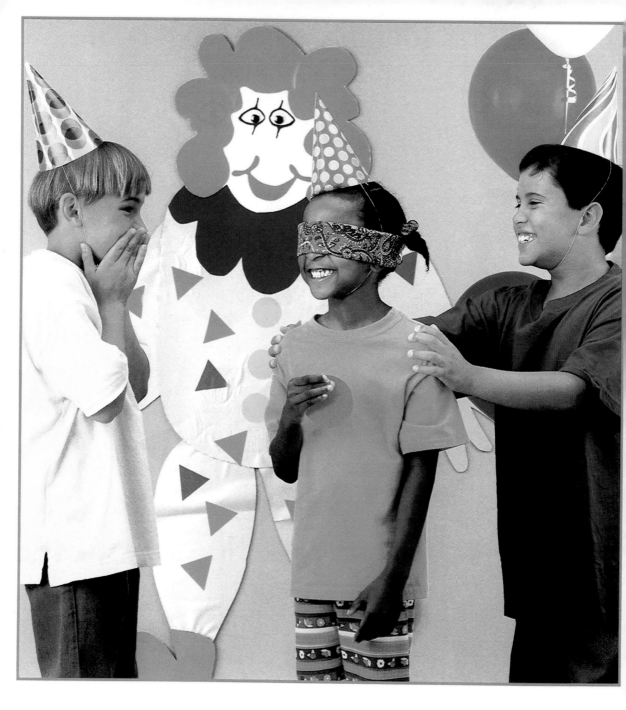

Spin, spin, spin.

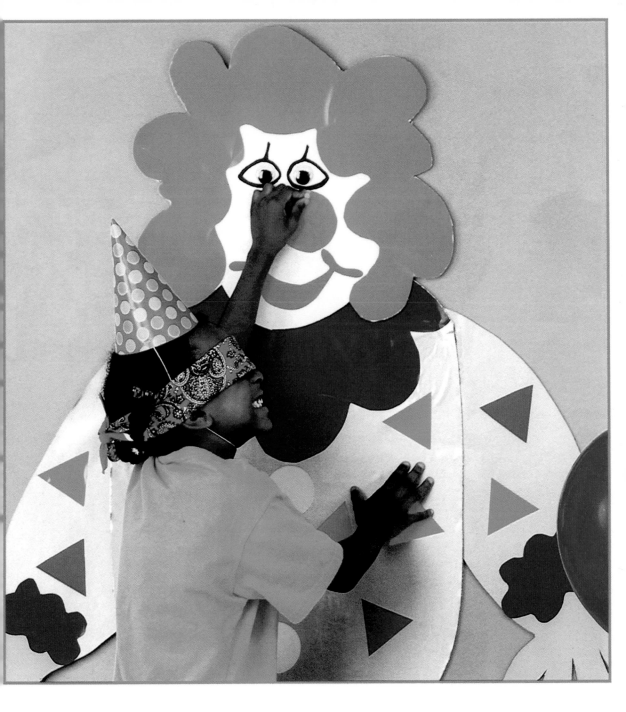

Put it on the face.

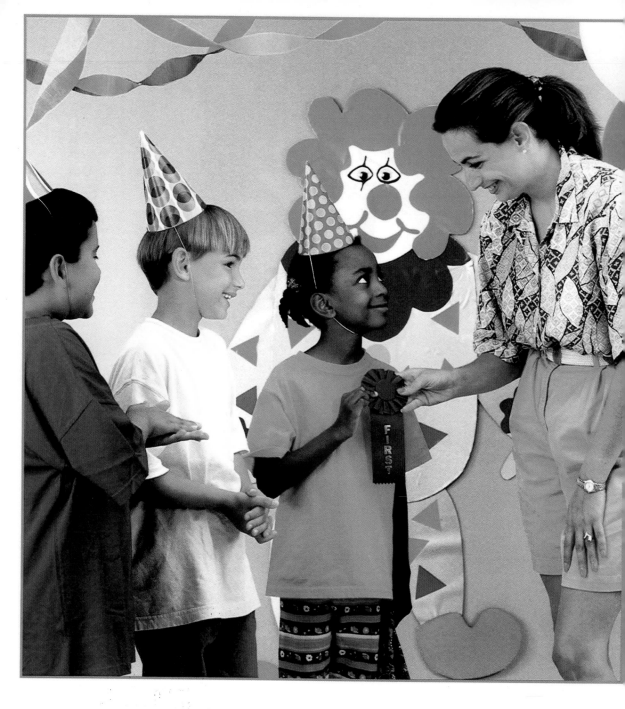

Pin it! You win!